Benediction

The woods are like cathedrals in the grey
November days—when the fires of Autumn
smoulder to a smoky haze. The beeches
stand like stone-grey pillars fading out of
sight—into aisles of shadow flecked with
gleams of golden light.

High above the dappled paths the arching
branches rise—and through their windows
shafts of glory strike down from the
skies,—glowing on the rich mosaics that
the leaves have made—yellow, russet,
red and green in grove and glen and
glade.

Do not miss November's beauty. Go and
see it now—before the winter closes in and
strips the last bare bough. Walk in Nature's
great cathedrals. Listen and you'll hear—
God pronounce His benediction on the
dying year.

Rest

Rest is nature's cure for minds and bodies
overtaxed. It's only when the pressures and
the tensions are relaxed—that she can do
her healing work, renewing health and
strength. Not quickly—not in haste, but in
her own time she at length—will repair the
ravages of all the stress and strain. Slowly,
gently, she will lead you back to life again.
Not by the prescription of a costly remedy—
but through rest: the secret of her simple
therapy.

This Their Legacy

Build up not out if build you must—and
spare the countryside—for this is England's
heritage and this is England's pride! The
primrose lanes of April and the bluebell
woods of May. The pastures bright with
buttercups, the banks and hedges gay—with
roses and with honeysuckle, thorn and
gorse and broom: the meadows and the
cliffside paths where honeyed heathers
bloom . . . Hold these things in trust for
generations yet to be. Keep them for our
children's children. This their legacy.

Peace, Be Still

The sea of life is wide and deep. I dare
not ask to be—sheltered always from the
currents of adversity . . . Though around
my little ship the giant waves break in
force—I must stand and learn to steer a
wise and steady course.

I must not pray for calmer seas—but for a
mind that knows—the quiet centre at the
heart of every storm that blows . . . May I
hear the Master's voice when winds blow
wild and shrill—speaking to me in the
tumult saying, Peace, be still.

Believing

Life is for living and joy is for giving—to all whom we meet as the days' path we tread . . . Hope is for lifting the eyes to the sunshine—facing the glow of the glory ahead.

Faith is believing. Faith is receiving—courage and strength as the dark road we plod . . . Prayer is for changing the tears and the torment into the peace and the comfort of God.

Another Lovely Day

With the first grey streak of light a bird
begins to sing—waking me as if to say
"Get up you lazy thing—can't you see the
rising sun has chased the stars away—and
that God is sending you another lovely
day ."

"There you lie, though problems press
and there is much to do, but I have a nest
to build. Oh yes, I'm busy too! And my food
to find, for it's the early bird that wins.
Yet I've time to sing to God before the
day begins ."

The Music of the Sea

There's a magic in the music of the restless
sea. There's a fascination in the endless
symphony—played upon the instruments of
wind and wave and spray—rising in
crescendo on a wild and stormy day—or

dying on a quiet note beneath the moon's
pale gleams. Never does the heart grow
weary of the changing themes—that swell
to angry tones or lull to moods of
somnolence—the everlasting orchestration
of the elements.

No Time For Tears

The dead leaves blow along the street. The
dying creepers fall. Some say it's a time for
tears, the saddest time of all, but I can
hear no sorrow in the sighing of the breeze—
or see no cause for lamentation in the
tattered trees.

This is Nature's wise provision. Things
must cease to grow—resting for a season
under ice and frost and snow—so they
will be ready for the moment of rebirth—
when God performs His miracle and
recreates the earth.

Waiting

Under the earth the bulbs lie deep—
buried in their winter sleep. Under the
frosts the seeds are sealed—in garden bed
and furrowed field.

Under a shroud of seeming death—they
wait for April's warming breath: iris,
tulips, crocuses, daffodils, anemones . . . In
the hard unyielding ground—the sapless
roots are locked and bound. Below the
crust of morning rime—Nature, dormant,
bides her time. Lilac, poppy, cherry,
may—await their resurrection day.

Take Heart

Take heart if things look hopeless. Take
heart and call to mind—that often when you
thought the worst—you turned a bend to
find—a happier prospect facing you—an
easier road, a brighter view.

Things seem to reach a climax—and when
you're near despair—there comes when least
expected, the answer to a prayer . . . Ends
prove to be beginnings. Have faith and play
your part. This hour may be the darkest
before the dawn. Take heart.

There All The Time

They were there all the time in the frozen
clay. They were down in the dark where
the thick frost lay, but I could not believe
they would come again—as I sought for
them there in the wintry lane.

And now they are here where my
snow-boots trod: primroses fresh from the
hand of God . . . A carpet of yellow and
green I see—mocking my incredulity.

Just like the blessings we long to find—
when we are troubled in heart and mind—
blessings like primroses hidden from
view—They were there all the time . . . but
we never knew.

The Sun

After many bitter weeks of ice and frost and
snow—the sun is like the smile of God upon
the world below. You lift your face to feel
its glow and as it shines on you—the glory
and the power of it you realise anew.

Suddenly there come these moments
when you are aware—of how wonderful
it is, that ball of fire up there—that draws
the green shoot from the dark where
winter's course has run—and with a joy
akin to worship you salute the sun.

Green Belt

Heaths and commons round our towns
make belts of greenery—where trees can
spread their boughs, where birds can
sing and man can see—the glory of the
open sky outstretched above his head,
walking where the unpaved earth is soft
beneath his tread.

Year by year the built-up roads reach
outwards to consume—the good and
precious land, where grasses blow and
wildflowers bloom . . . where town joins
town with no sweet stream of air to flow
between—men live and die and never see
that touch of living green—that in places
unconfined, rests the eye and calms the mind.

Always a Surprise

We know it's going to happen but it's
always a surprise—when green tips poke out
of the earth and point towards the skies . . .
First the dainty snowdrop, then the crocus
white and gold—then the early daffodils
preparing to unfold.

At the gates of Lent they stand, the heralds
of the Spring—before the blackbird and the
thrushes really start to sing . . . While winter
fires still crackle and its fogs hang in the
air—they seem to come up overnight and
take us unaware.

We never grow accustomed to this annual
miracle. Year by year we see it but it's
always wonderful. We never quite believe
it till it's there before our eyes. Every
year it happens but it's always a surprise.

This Lovely World

Once again the lilac tassels flutter in the
breeze—and the green leaves open out upon
the budding trees. There are new lambs in
the field and fledglings in the nest—as the
old earth wakes once more out of its
winter rest.

In the orchards blossom breaks in white
and rosy spray. Gardens, parks and cottage
plots are glorious and gay—with beds of
tulips, pink and scarlet blazing rich and
bold—and wallflowers massed in glowing
shades of amber, wine and gold.

In the woods the bluebells make a carpet
thick and bright. The hawthorns in the
hedges are bedecked in bridal white—and
the yellow banners of laburnums are
unfurled . . . How thankful we should be
for this our good and lovely world!

The Answer

The corn has ripened in the fields—and
once again the good earth yields—a wealth
of grain to meet man's need: the barn
to fill, the towns to feed.

When the golden harvest tide—rolls across
the countryside—we see the rich beneficence
of a loving Providence . . . Year by year for
this we pray. Throughout the world by
night and day—the universal prayer is
said: Give us this day our daily bread.

Best Of All

I love the April daffodils, the irises of May.
I love June's gift of roses and the smell of
new mown hay. I love the solemn beauty
of the lilies of July—and the blue
delphiniums that match the summer sky.

. . . I love to see the rose-pink spires of
August hollyhocks—high above the
dahlias, the asters and the phlox; but best of
all I love September with its mellow days:
the month that brings the ripened berries
and the fruited sprays. Chrysanthemums—
and creepers turning red upon the wall. The
climax of the gardener's year; to me the
best of all.